MW01205979

Law of Attraction

Secrets to manifesting more of what you want and less of what you don't

Manhardeep Singh

Contents

Part - 1   1

1. Unity Domain   5

2. Nature and Contact   9

3. Mirror Drill   13

4. Great Character Traits   17

Conclusion   23

Part - 2   25

5. Connect   27

6. Communicate   31

7. Sharing   37

8. Be Kind to Yourself   43

Conclusion   51

Part - 3   53

9. Disconnected Mentality   55

10. Dread of being Declined   63

11. Not being compatible   67

12. Ways to connect   73

Conclusion   81

What next?   83

Part - 1

Achieving Oneness through Unison

Developing true union with others with one accord of harmony.

The very first step to open the door and let the unleashed power in is to enter into the state of unity. Now, no one may pressure you into a state of unity. It can only be felt by conscious choice. This choice includes both mental and emotional sides.

The mental choice calls for choosing to view the world through the lens of interconnection, to see yourself as piece of a greater body, and to assume the new level of responsibility that develops from that position. The emotional option is to by choice tune in to this ever-present connection and to feel it as joy.

To truly master unity, both the mental and emotional sides must be integrated. You need to realize the truth of unity, as well as feel your loving connection with others.

If you only have the mental side of the unity, you'll understand and concur with the logic of unity. However, you will not truly get it intuitively. You'll lack the drive to transform your realizations into direct actions.

If you only have the emotional side, you'll intuitively feel that we are all associated at some level, yet you'll lack a reasonable reality to comprehend it. You'll feel happy at times, yet you'll struggle with blending that into all areas of life.

When building up a sense of unity, it's helpful to start by centering on either the mental or the emotional side, depending upon whether you prefer your system of logic or intuition.

Start with whichever side you prefer and afterwards use your progress to research the other side. You can also shift back and forth between both the sides in order to advance them together.

In the following chapters, you will find specific exercises you can utilize to formulate and expand your experience of unity. A few of these deal with the mental side, while others center on the emotional side.

CHAPTER 1

Unity Domain

ALLOW 10 MINUTES TO SIT QUIET, RELAX, AND SCARCELY THINK OF WHAT IT MIGHT BE LIKE TO LIVE IN A WORLD WHERE EVERYBODY LIVES LINED UP WITH UNITY.

Have A Fresh Look

Imagine a world where all individuals feel happy and connected to everyone. Imagine a place where collaboration replaces competition. What would it be like to walk down the street, walk around so many strangers and feel that they are all close loved ones?

How would individuals function in a world where the "we" mentality replaces the "me" thinking, where benefitting does not occur at the expense of others and where everyone accepts personal responsibility for the wellbeing of all?

In this domain of unity, you can always expect fair treatment, regardless of skin color, gender or sexual orientation.

If you need help with anything, you can turn to anyone at any time and you will be treated as a loved one. Belief in individual growth at the expense of other people is completely foreign. The mantra of the human race is, "We are all in this collectively."

This new domain has no weapons, no prison and no national boundaries. There was no fury or state of war.

Individuals still have conflicts; however, they resolve them by joining forces to uncover the truth, treating each individual with consideration and thoughtfulness.

Let your mind and emotions move freely through the unity domain. Imagine what it would be like to live there. Pay attention to how you experience your environment.

Even if this is a fantasy drill, it can deepen your understanding of unity. Even in real life, you can go through some of these benefits when you start on the line of unity.

If you treat others with cooperation, honesty and consideration, you are likely to receive the same treatment from each other. If you treat everyone as a friend or loved one, you will often find that they react the same way.

Over time, you will attract more people who line up with unity, allowing you to create a personal community of unity in your own life.

CHAPTER 2

Nature and Contact

SPENDING A LITTLE TIME IN NATURE AND GETTING SOME CONTACT IS AMONG THE EASIEST THINGS YOU ARE ABLE TO DO TO FEEL UNITY.

Find Your Roots

Even if you can take out only an hour or less, use it to get away from city life and reconnect with your roots. Keep an eye out for animals. Touch the tree. Feel the wind on your face.

Realize that you are not separate from nature and that it is part of you. You are not a stranger to these environments - you really are meant to be here. Watch how wonderful it is to stop working, to stop thinking and to simply be with the plants and animals.

Reconnect with the reality that you're part of the kingdom of animals. Imagine a path up the side of a mountain with an amazing view of a beautiful canyon. You sat there solely for 60 minutes taking in the sunset while savoring a calm, meditative state. You feel so peaceful that you stay put till the last possible moment, leaving hardly enough light to make it back down the path before it was too black to see. Such experiences are an excellent way to reload the emotional side of our unity experiences.

A truly satisfying way to experience unity is to make loving physical contact with other willing individuals. Cuddle your partner in a spoon position. Hold a youngster in your lap. Rock a baby. Don't say anything - it's just the experience to savor to recognize the link between you.

As you maintain physical contact, imagine expanding your consciousness to embrace other individual's body. Say the words in your mind that I am you. No separation, no difference between you. You both fade into each other and you share unique awareness.

Savor this feeling of complete connection, unhampered by any thoughts of detachment. Don't simply imagine you're one; recognize you're one. As well as bringing on a feeling of unity, physical contact may likewise intensify your intimate link with another individual, a link that might hold on even after you physically let go of them.

As this bond with one person grows, the way you treat other people will gradually change. Individuals who love nature act more thoughtfully and compassionately.

Linking up with animals may induce a state of unity too.

CHAPTER 3

Mirror Drill

PICK OUT A RANDOM INDIVIDUAL, SUCH
AS AN ACQUAINTANCE, FELLOW WORKER,
OR FAMOUS PERSON. HOW WOULD YOU
DISTINGUISH THIS INDIVIDUAL?

Look At Yourself

Make a small list of the most important characteristics of this person. Then put a plus sign (+) next to the characteristics you like and a subtraction sign (-) next to those you do not.

Now consider the list you have produced, and read it back to yourself.

This time, however, think from a position where you are dealing with a list of characteristics others compiled to describe you. You will probably gain some new perspective about yourself because you will realize that it is an unbiased representation of what you love and have disapproval for most about yourself.

I have recommended this mirror drill to many individuals around the world, and those who have implemented it are amazed at what it reveals. I recommend you try it for yourself. It only takes a few moments and will help you recognize that other people are not very different from you.

We often praise others for what we love so much about us and condemn the characteristics we protest against. By the way, did I bring up what a beautiful, bright, and loving individual you are?

Unity is one of the most ambitious things to apply consistently as large part of the world is still lined up with detachment.

An essential part of unity is the ability to dispel thoughts of detachment and allow your awareness to expand beyond the limits of your own importance. The more your own importance controls your consciousness, the more you automatically detach yourself from the people around you.

CHAPTER 4

Great Character Traits

A PERSON WITH GOOD PERSONALITY TRAITS IN CHARGE OF HIS OWN LIFE, RECOGNIZES HIS GOAL AND VISION AND IS COMMITTED TO SEE THAT IT HAPPENS.

Great Character Traits

A person with good personality traits trains to be an effective communicator and has the power to influence others with his words and actions. Individuals respect him because he is caring and trustworthy. Due to his nature, he is able to achieve his goals with the help of other people and at the same time help them increase their self-confidence and improve their self-esteem.

You can't pretend to be charming, because time, event and situation will show if you really have it. Building a good reputation takes time. You were not born with it, but you gain it through training, experience and a strong vision, or the desire to be a worthy individual for yourself and those around you.

Here are some of the traits that comprise a person described above:

Foresight

Whatever your position in life is, you must have a vision. Once you have mastered this, you must use it in your life. Individuals can tell an individual with a vision. It shows how you drive and your commitment to growth, innovation and success.

Discipline and centered

You show this in your day-to-day discipline and how you focus on everyday work to improve productivity and performance. It is in your focus and determination to discover resolutions and have the courage to take risks.

Bearing favorable qualities and mental attitude

Individuals love and imitate other people who show confidence, determination and assertiveness. Followers will move towards people who can do important things despite failures and challenges.

Great communication

Your utilization of language is crucial. What and how you verbalize or deliver your message tell other people who you are. Learn to utilize words that affect and inspire other people. Words have the force to produce emotions and move individuals to take action.

Truthful

Use honesty and reality in your dealings but pay attention to other's feelings and personal values. Make it your path in your daily interactions.

Compromising

You need to adjust your techniques and change your priorities without compromising your principles and values when needed. Specific situations justify different actions and there must be the capacity for change and adaptation.

Modest and humble

You don't have to control other people with your position. If you want to have an admirable attitude, practice modesty and show compassion. Respect other people as they are and listen to their opinions. The way you treat other people reflects your ethical fiber.

Conclusion

I wish I could state I always act from a state of unity, but that wouldn't be reality. I've been at that place intellectually, emotionally, and spiritually; and I understand it's a beautiful place to be. When I am at my most beneficial, I've the clarity to consciously embrace unity. Regrettably, I'm not forever at my most beneficial.

Don't beat yourself up if you discover it hard to accomplish and hold the state of unity. It's adequate for now that you're mindful of the idea. When you feel the time is correct, you are able to consciously start working to better your alignment with unity.

Part - 2

ATTRACTING AUTHENTIC AFFECTION

Making Daily Decisions To Become More Connected.

Affection is an emotion, of course, but it is much more than that. One of the important choices you will face in each encounter is to either draw close or avoid. You can try to connect with individuals or retreat from them. You can get involved in your daily work or you may dillydally. You can get closer to any individual, place, or object to connect, or you can stay away.

The decision to connect is the core of affection. You are forced to make connection choices every day. Through your actions, you choose what to connect with and what to avoid. If you want to grow consciously, you must choose which connections to strengthen and which to let soften.

Such choices ultimately determine the shape of your life. In the long run, your life will be an expression of what you choose to connect with.

CHAPTER 5

Connect

IN ORDER TO DEVELOP AS A HUMAN, YOU HAVE TO MASTER THE ARTISTRY OF FORMING CONNECTIONS.

Associate

To connect means giving something your care, consideration and to engage with it. In addition to connecting with individuals, you can connect with groups, objects, places, thoughts, values, and actions. Creating a connection calls for nothing but your tending. Think of your mother. Think of democracy. Think of your favorite song. Be present and pay attention to something and you are able to connect with it.

Do you remember the first time you learned about the physical world as a child? You looked around and observed things that caught your eye. Then you went to them, grabbed them and started playing with them. You got to know your environment through direct practical experience. If you found something you didn't like, you tried to avoid it in the future. When you discovered something you admire, you gave more attention to it. Occasionally, your focus will bring you into a state of affection.

As adults, we have always been blank about the best way to satisfy our desires is to go directly for what fascinates us and engage with it straight off.

Instead, we create all sorts of goofy principles that limit our ability to take responsibility for what we want. We can't start a business because it's so dangerous. We can't talk to that person because we're already in a relationship. We cannot examine other belief systems because they are forbidden by our religion today.

Such principles are rooted in fear and disconnection and have no place in the life story of conscious development. If you commit to living consciously, you will often find that you struggle with principles. If you want to more loving, you have to be wishing to connect.

A great deal of my most valuable development happened when I decided to connect with something important to me in any event, when others disagreed with my determination.

To find and develop, you must allow to associate with what you wish and to disconnect from what you don't wish. Nobody might give you that opportunity. It's your right as a human. You don't need anyone's permission to choose which associations are beneficial for you.

It ultimately depends on you to initiate the drive to connect with what you wish and to turn off from what you don't wish. By deliberately showing up at associations that vibe instinctively right to you, you direct yourself into the right place with the rationale of affection.

Chapter 6

Communicate

COMMUNICATING IS THE MEANS THROUGH WHICH WE CONVEY AFFECTION.

Get In Touch

The root of the word communicate signifies "common," and it's normal to accept that once we speak with someone, we look for something we bear in common. Discovering commonalities is essentially how we produce new associations.

You communicate effectively by first and foremost connecting with the familiar and afterwards broadening into the new. At the point when you meet another person, the initial move is to figure out your shared concerns, values, and mental attitude. This creates a fundamental adherence of trust and friendship.

The accompanying measure is to explore and gain from your disparities. People who are excessively disparate from you are difficult to bond with, and the individuals who are too similar to you can't teach you a great deal. The most helpful connections supply sufficient common ground to forge a strong bond while also arousing development in new directions.

The most profound type of communication is up close and face-to-face discussion. This allows you to figure out the content as well as the vocal aspects along with non-verbal cues from body language. You'll generally have a lot better relationship with people when you communicate in the flesh as opposed to by phone or email.

Exceptional communication skills take time to formulate. The more you practice, the better you'll become. While there are specific strategies you might learn, like grinning, sustaining an open stance, and attaining eye contact, remember that the primary motivation behind conveying is to deliver a connection with the other person. When you've a specific plan as a primary agenda in mind like persuasion, training, or entertainment, your initial move is to establish a bond.

Phenomenal public speakers, teachers, and performers try to break the ice and connect with their audiences first of all; only after this has been achieved do they go into their content material.

True communication calls for mutual understanding established in affection and faith; any other way, you can't, in actuality, share truth with others.

It isn't enough to express your real thoughts and assume others comprehend and acknowledge what you're expressing, nor is it sufficient to listen well and expect you to comprehend what is expressed. To communicate effectively, there should be some bond between talker and audience.

There are few pleasures in life over the experience of conscious communicating with another person. No self-importance games, misleading fronts, or manipulative moves are used. The two individuals just wish to connect with each other to learn and develop.

At the point when you've gone through such uncovered, conscious communicating with another human, it's hard to go with anything less.

CHAPTER 7

Sharing

SHARING IS THE DEEP SENSATION OF BONDING
THAT BRINGS ABOUT THE EMOTIONAL SIDE
OF AFFECTION. IT'S THE DELECTABLE FEELING
OF COMPLETENESS THAT STEMS FROM
PORTIONING OUT OUR REAL SELVES.

A Part of You

Think about your relationship with another
person. Where does it in actuality exist? It
doesn't exist anywhere in the outside world.
You can't simply point towards it and say, "This
is our relationship right here." It lives strictly
inside your thoughts alone.

In this manner, your relationship with another person is anything that you accept it is. Your idea makes the relationship significant. If you stop to believe in it, for every single down-to-earth reason, it no more exists. The substantial residue could remain on, similar to a particular living arrangement, yet the real human connection would get abandoned.

When you understand that there's no such thing as an external relationship and that all such associations live totally in your brain, you will know the actual point of relationships is self exploration.

When you communicate in any manner, you are, in reality, exploring various aspects of yourself. When you feel a rich feeling of imparting to another individual, you are actually connecting significantly with a vital piece of yourself.

By sharing with others, you find how to love yourself more. I typically receive various emails of reviews through my website: www.manhardeep.com. A ton of it comes from people who've never met me face to face, nor have they at any point had any conversation with me.

All this is because of the things I've shared through my books and blog. Many trust me to be a dear friend as they understand so much about me, so they get in contact with me from the place as if we share a deep bond. In their beginning message, they share with me matters about themselves which they won't even tell their mates.

In their brains, they've gone through such a strong communion with me over a time span of weeks or months that they feel easy discussing their darkest secrets. Naturally, I put forth a valiant effort to regard such a relationship in the caring way in which they are offered up.

From my own inward position, no different either way, a much more strong shift has occurred. I notice that as I've strengthened my own offering to myself by examining my contemplations on paper, my external world has changed over to mirror that internal development.

As opposed to opening with shallow chatter, people start discussions with me by immediately diving into issues of great significance to them. Indeed, even adolescents speak to me in this way. The more I share with myself within, the richer my connections with others become.

These days, my life brims over with opportunities for sound human association. For quite a while, I've seen plentiful proof that our associations with others resonate between our inward associations with assorted pieces of ourselves. Assuming you've inconvenience associating with people on the outside, it very well may be because you're not sharing with yourself on the inside.

When you find how to feel fondly connected on the inside, you'll find it a lot less complex to form a bond with others.

The incredible news is that when you appreciate that all connections are inside, you can intentionally change how you see them and change how they go, too. On the off chance that you feel detached with your genuine self, you can expect that your own connections should experience the ill effects of a distinction, as well. If you wish your connections to be seriously cherishing and accepting, find how to adore and live with more facets of yourself.

Cherishing yourself absolutely and genuinely is the result of a cognizant determination. You can show up at this decision at every moment each day. You don't have to fulfill any circumstances or satisfy any rules. Nonetheless, to settle on this decision deliberately, you need to get to know yourself. Despite what disguised characteristics you go over, you're as yet deserving of affection.

CHAPTER 8

Be Kind to Yourself

I'VE ALWAYS REALIZED THE IMPORTANCE OF
KINDNESS, BUT I'VE ALWAYS CENTERED ON
KINDNESS TO OTHER PEOPLE. I HAD NEVER
CONSIDERED KINDNESS TOWARD MYSELF.

Be Easy

I started with how it feels to have someone
be kind to you. I grasp that inclination. It's
delicate and comfortable and holding. In any
case, I'm not the one to call forward that kind
of feeling in myself. I thought about how it feels
to be kind - the feelings that take off inside you
while you're thinking about another individual;
care and gentleness. I don't habitually feel such

feelings while managing myself. This prompts me to address whether I'm ever distinctly kind to myself and how my life may be changed in the event that I explicitly paid myself a little kind consideration.

I've been considering the way that you can be kind to yourself and the advantages of doing as such. The following are a couple of my hints.

It's vital to show patience towards yourself on the off chance that you're combating with an endeavor. An evening or two ago I was going to a yoga class. It was warm and tacky, and I was over and over, not able to deal with my postures as my hands continued to slip. I was very irritated with myself. My instructor advised me that a few days I'd be better at it than other days. Every so often my movement would be firmer than on others and that it was anything but a competition with myself.

Now I imagine: "What if I had expressed that to myself and not depended on the instructor to redirect me from the cruel way of behaving towards myself?" Impatience has an approach to driving toward diminished self-respect and a terrible state of mind. It's in like manner something we will frown over; becoming trapped in the negative past as opposed to valuing the present time and place. Stay patient and you'll wipe the slate clean in your life.

Everyone has self-talk or self-chatter. Occasionally it's positive and occasionally it's damaging (or very damaging). Do you state things to yourself like: "you moron" or "how could you have possibly done that?" Do you state things to yourself that you wouldn't state to other people? Is what you state to yourself kind?

I understand that if somebody stated directly to me some of the lectures that I give myself, I'd be exceedingly hurt. So why is it okay for me to make such remarks to myself? For a lot of reasons it's great to try to be aware of damaging self-talk and to turn it around. Through awareness one may take action. In the case of "kindness to self", I think it's crucial to alter sinister to words and tones into sentences that you'd feel comfortable utilizing with somebody else. Gracious words, kind words, make you feel great or better or even accepted.

When matters are tough or you're combating with something, encouragement is a marvellous means of presenting you a boost. But, does encouragement have to come from somebody externally? I think we ought to always have enough favourable belief in ourselves to carry us through. Belief is empowering.

Forgiveness is often not simple. Among the moves toward accomplishing forgiveness is self-forgiveness. Thus, in the event that we don't get that right, we're "damned" in endeavors to forgive others. It is thoughtful to Forgive yourself. It is thoughtful to Forgive others.

Acts of kindness call for giving - whether it's material or time or power of some sorts. Are you generous towards yourself? I believe it's critical to treat yourself with matters you enjoy (even if it's only a bath in pretty oils) and gifts.

Everyone needs to get some time for themselves, be it reading or going to a class or lunch with a friend. You provide for others to rejuvenate them. You're similarly as deserving of and needing rejuvenation. Rejuvenation is critical to accomplishment. Plus, you can't provide to others, what you don't have a lot for yourself first.

Kindness, similarly, calls for listening. Do you pay attention to yourself? Do you notice what your body, heart and soul are saying?

It's crucial to rest if you're worn out, to have some time off if you've been mentally overworking, and to make modifications if you're dissatisfied, to search for help if you want it. It's another key to achievement and happiness. Attentiveness to yourself is important for an ideal life journey.

With kindness, one delivers a space for and lets another individual be themselves and go through their emotions. Allowing yourself to feel terrible or damaging emotions helps with pushing ahead - insofar as you can handle them. If you keep concealing them, they draw you descending and in reverse. You can be empathetic and feel for yourself without wallowing in self-pity.

Kindness might require the offering of guidance or ideas. So it's a matter of having control over issues, realizing your expectation and afterward applying it (benevolently!). A step toward development.

If you consider it, is everybody not worthy of kindness? So then also are you.

Conclusion

All humans are made with the natural need to give and get affection. We're made in affection which shapes the premise of our divine spiritual selves, and of our genuinely manifested life. Indeed, even the many limits that we experience in our early lives don't eliminate warmth from our spiritual center, since it's the substance of who we are.

The quality of affection is truly universal - as it literally transcends people, nations and religions. Affection is truly the universal language of this world and individuals from all different walks of life acknowledge it for what it truly is and comprehend the power that is in it. Surrounding yourself with love brings favorable energy into your life.

Part - 3

ROADBLOCKS TO AFFECTION

Removing the setbacks in Love

Certain issues may prevent you from easily forming new connections or intensifying existing ones, trapping you in a never-ending state of disconnection. Here are a few of the most basic roadblocks that keep you from being in alignment with affection.

CHAPTER 9

Disconnected Mentality

CONSCIOUSLY CONNECTING BECOMES
DIFFICULT WHEN YOUR MIND IS CLUTTERED
WITH THOUGHTS THAT KEEP YOU
DISCONNECTED.

The Wrong Mindset

A belief in detachment becomes self-fulfilling. A disconnected mind breeds behaviours that reward a disconnected way of life. Instead of reaching out to people with love, you hold back. Instead of giving someone a hug, you settle for a handshake. Rather than actively initiating a conversation, you wait for the other person to make the first move.

It is important to recognize that the notion that everyone is a completely separate being from you is an unprovable assumption. Do you believe that the other dream personas are separate and distinct when you're sleeping and having a dream? You most likely make that assumption while sleeping, but when you wake up, you know it's not true. Those dream personas are simply brain projections. They exist entirely within you, not apart from you.

What if you brought that same mindset into your waking life?

There is no hard and fast rule that says you must assume everyone is different from you. Something magical happens when you imagine that everyone else is a part of you, just like one of your own dream personas. The first thing you notice is that there are no strangers.

There are no insignificant people in your reality. Because everyone is a part of you, everyone has something to teach you. Enjoying another person becomes the same as enjoying a part of yourself.

Because all parts of you deserve affection, no human is unworthy of it either. Loving others and loving yourself are, in the end, the same thing.

I met a curious person by chance in my early adult years. I discovered myself opening up to her really well during one of our first conversations. I had no idea why, but I felt completely safe with her and trusted her implicitly. We became very close friends very quickly, and I mean that literally. I'd never experienced such a strong and rapid bonding with another person before.

Over the course of several weeks, I noticed that this woman was able to find a similar level of compatibility with almost everyone she met. Within the first 10 minutes of conversation, complete strangers would begin telling her their life story. When I asked how this was happening, she explained that it was the result of a special mentality she had about people.

She stated that she knew in her heart that we are all parts of the same whole. She didn't have to make new connections with people. She'd simply tap into the connection she assumed was already in place. Her mentality aligned her with affection because she saw everyone as being fondly connected to her.

This was a completely foreign concept to me. I was certain we were all single individuals. Making a genuine connection with someone required time, common interests, personal rapport, and a bit of luck. People occasionally connected, and sometimes they didn't.

Nonetheless, I couldn't deny this woman's results.

I finally got over my disbelief and attempted that I was already connected to everyone else. I can't say it was easy to do this consistently, but the more I thought about it, the more true it became. Emotionally, I became a more loving person. I began making new friends much more easily, and my social life reached new heights. Occasionally, when I met someone for the first time, I knew we'd be great friends right away. Unconsciously, I began interacting with people I'd just met as if we'd known each other for a long time, and I noticed they frequently responded in a similar manner.

You can easily connect with people by tuning in to the connection that already exists. Instead of being forced to break the ice with someone, assume there is no ice. You're already affiliated on some level. As you become more aligned with this viewpoint, you may find that complete strangers approach you to strike up a conversation. When you are fondly connected to others, you will frequently notice that others care for you in the same way.

This is a skill that can be developed with time and practise. You don't have to accept the doctrine underlying this concept to benefit from it. You can put it to use simply by using your imagination.

Imagine that each person you meet is already inherently connected to you the next time you're with a group of people. Assume the affectionate bond already exists, and observe what happens.

CHAPTER 10

Dread of being Declined

DREAD OF REJECTION MAKES SMALL SOCIAL FUNDAMENTAL INTERACTION SEEM LIKE MAMMOTH THREATS.

Stave off Fear

Such dread creates feelings of vacancy, aloneness, and reclusiveness, draining you of the positive desire to connect with others and pushing you out of alignment with affection.

Is there anything inherently wrong with approaching another person and saying, "My name is Joe, and I'd like to introduce myself. You appear to be someone I've never met before. What is your name?"

The other person may initially react as if you are attempting to sell them something, but they will frequently give you the benefit of the doubt and allow the conversation to continue. In the worst-case scenario, nothing happens.

The best-case scenario is that you make a fascinating new life acquaintance. How many times can you risk something like that? When you open your heart and communicate with affection, you're bound to meet others who respond in kind.

The irony is that when you're feeling disconnected from something, connecting with people is the cure.

It's unlikely that you'll feel blue in the first place if you spend more time with positive, cheerful, and interesting people.

In reality, your disconnect from others indicates that you have disconnected from the most beneficial parts of yourself.

You are a worthy person. When you avoid connecting out of fear of rejection, you deny others the chance to get to know you.

Many people would welcome the opportunity to contact you. They want someone to understand them, someone to remind them that they are not alone.

When you connect with people, you are giving them exactly what they want. Extending socially does involve some risk, but the long-term benefits are so great that the only way to fail is to never try.

CHAPTER 11

Not being compatible

WHILE IT'S IMAGINABLE TO CONNECT WITH
LITERALLY ANYBODY ON A SOULFUL LEVEL,
IT'S SIMPLER TO COMMUNICATE WITH THOSE
WHO BEAR SOMETHING IN COMMON WITH

YOU.

Similarities

A shared way of life, shared values, and
a similar disposition grease the wheels of
communication, making it easier to form new
connections and strengthen existing ones.

When looking for new connections to enrich
your life, look for people who are a good fit for

you, especially in terms of characters, values, and mental attitude.

Have you ever found yourself nodding along while someone else is speaking, even if you disagree with everything they're saying?

You understand that if you speak up and express your true feelings, it will only lead to a pointless debate. This is a common occurrence when we communicate with people whose values differ from ours. When basic rapport is lacking, communication becomes difficult, misinterpretations increase, and it is difficult to connect with reality and affection.

Your compatibility preferences will undoubtedly change as you grow older. Nobody is to blame. Allow yourself to let go of any group, individual, job, or activity that no longer resonates with you, and you'll soon attract more opportunities that are a good fit for you.

If you feel it's time to move on, do so with love. Take your interaction from the level of direct interaction to the level of cherished memory. Then file that memory away and prepare for something new.

The process of letting go can be extremely difficult, but it is an essential part of personal development. When you fail to let go of incompatibilities in your life, you settle for permissiveness and prevent compatible new relationships from forming.

You also create an even greater disconnect within yourself. Permissiveness is an act of opposition to affection, not an act of affection.

When you fill your life with compatible associations, something very powerful happens. First and foremost, you will feel warmly supported and encouraged to express yourself authentically. Second, because you know you have a solid foundation to fall back on, you'll find it easier to associate with people who would otherwise be completely incompatible with you.

For example, Christ may have communicated with people who held very different values than his, but he spent a lot of time with the twelve apostles who defended and believed in him.

Perhaps Judas wasn't the best of friends, but eleven out of twelve isn't bad! How would you feel if you had twelve devoted followers who referred to you as Lord and Master and saw you as their teacher and Redeemer? Do you think it would allow you to branch out and connect with less fear and hesitancy? Do you think it would help you stay aligned with affection?

Don't wait for loving connections to knock on your door. Get out there and consciously create them.

CHAPTER 12

Ways to connect

LIKE ANY OTHER ACQUIRED ABILITY, GREAT COMMUNICATING SKILLS TAKE PRACTICE TO DEVELOP.

Some Help

If you feel awkward socially and have trouble connecting with others, the problem could be a lack of experience. Great communication skills, like any other acquired skill, require practise to develop. With practise, you'll become more at ease in a variety of social situations, and once you're at ease, you'll be able to express yourself naturally.

Relaxation is the foundation of effective communication. When you are completely at ease with yourself, your self-importance fades into the background. You aren't preoccupied with how you appear, how you sound, or what other people think of you.

You're concentrating on the matters you're discussing and the people you're speaking with.

To develop your social skills, you must create conditions that allow your natural communication style to emerge. Starting with the most compatible people you can find is one of the best ways to do so. Develop your skills within that group, and then use your connections to expand into other areas where you aren't as easily found. For example, a young man who is shy around women may notice that he communicates naturally with other players in a net game.

To gain experience with women, he may focus on getting to know a few of the females in the game, even if they are thousands of miles away. Then, move some of those friendships to e-mail and phone calls to deepen them. When he is comfortable with those associations, he may consider joining a local gaming club and interacting with women in person. You can vastly improve your social skills by starting with a well-matched base and working to build your connections.

Here's a simple exercise that will improve your ability to connect. Consider someone you already know and like. If you can't think of anyone, think of someone you admire or respect. Consider that person and then decide to send affection to that person. Consider your affection to be positive energy flowing out of you. Make use of the existing link between you. Recognize that you are both components of the same whole. Hold that thought for a moment and notice how good it feels.

Now try this: think of a mundane object for which you have no strong feelings, such as a pencil. Choose something within reach and grab it. Consider it, and become aware of the intangible link that already exists between you and this thing. Consider this to be a part of you. Send your affection energy to that thing and tell it, "I love you," and "You're beautiful." This may appear unusual, but it still feels fantastic. What else can you love if you can love something ordinary?

You can truly fall in love with anything. Affection is not by chance. The goal is to persuade you to take a position that makes it easier to give and receive affection. It's easier to acknowledge affection as something that already exists rather than assuming you have to create it from scratch.

Sharing something with others is one of the simplest ways to connect with them. Participate in a conversation, exchange of experiences, stories, laughter, and a meal. Life is full of opportunities to share interesting moments with others. Don't be afraid to go first. If you extend a lunch invitation, the other person may decline. Don't let that discourage you. Simply make the same offer to someone else, and you'll soon find someone who appreciates your friendly advances.

Engulfing yourself in an activity with another person, such as going on a date, to a party, or on a holiday together, is a popular type of sharing. This may result in long-lasting memories that help to cement the bond. Sharing fosters trust, and trust fosters stronger bonds.

Take a straightforward approach. This technique requires a little bravery, but when it works, it works exceptionally well. The direct approach entails verbally expressing your affection for another person. Simply make a direct statement like, "You know... you're a truly great friend," during a conversation. Unless there is some sort of fundamental animosity between the two of you, the other person will almost always respond in a similar manner.

You'll probably notice that your association has reached a new level after venting such feelings. If you don't feel comfortable being overly gooey, you can always go for something more subtle. A handshake and a genuine smile are also ways to recognise your connection.

A different way to connect with others is to express genuine admiration for them. Recognize the other person for a recent accomplishment. Take note of a special talent or skill that you admire, or simply share a small detail that moves you. Only do this if you are truly moved. Never provide false praise in an attempt to manipulate others.

The final method of connecting is to express gratitude to the other person. It's sometimes easiest to tap into those feelings by imagining your life without him or her. What would you miss if this person was no longer in the picture?

You can also use appreciation on a larger scale. What about your family, community, country, or planet makes you grateful? What would you miss if they were no longer there? When you are grateful for your community, you will find it much easier to associate with other residents, as this is a way of effectively observing the already existing association.

Conclusion

Affection is the principle that allows you to gradually discover your true self. You do this by making connections with other people and then communicating with them to explore those bonds.

The more you become involved with the world around you, the better your alignment with affection will be. The belief that you are completely separate from everyone else is an illusion. Consider your relationships as outside projections of your true self, and you'll see that the goal of each is to teach you how to love yourself from the inside out.

When you communicate with another person, you are truly exploring the depths of your own consciousness, as this is where all of your relationships reside. When you learn to love everyone and everything, you become more in tune with your true self. There is no true distinction between loving other people and loving yourself; the two are inseparably linked.

What next?

When reality, affection, and power might are all in sync, the dominant idea in personal development emerges: intelligence. Next in the series, learn how to construct your fortress of success by discovering the balance in your aptitude.

About Author

Manhardeep Singh is an India-based best-selling author, motivational speaker, and handwriting analyst. Gaining from the experience of one-on-one counseling sessions, Manhardeep pens down self-help books. His writings are focused on the topics of handwriting analysis and bring the best out of life.

Manhardeep Singh has a Masters degree in Business Administration. He regularly writes articles in his blog www.manhardeep.com

Made in United States
Troutdale, OR
04/11/2024

19122097R00050